SHARKS SET II

LANTERN SHARKS

Adam G. Klein

ABDO Publishing Company

visit us at
www.abdopub.com

Published by ABDO Publishing Company, 4940 Viking Drive, Edina, Minnesota 55435.
Copyright © 2006 by Abdo Consulting Group, Inc. International copyrights reserved in all
countries. No part of this book may be reproduced in any form without written permission from
the publisher. The Checkerboard Library™ is a trademark and logo of ABDO Publishing
Company.

Printed in the United States.

Cover Photo: Peter Arnold
Interior Photos: © Espen Rekdel / SeaPics.com p. 13; © Florian Graner / SeaPics.com pp. 5, 9,
    17; © Jeff Rotman / SeaPics.com pp. 10-11, 15, 18-19; © Rudie Kuiter / SeaPics.com p. 21;
    Uko Gorter pp. 6-7

Series Coordinator: Heidi M. Dahmes
Editors: Heidi M. Dahmes, Stephanie Hedlund
Art Direction: Neil Klinepier

Library of Congress Cataloging-in-Publication Data

Klein, Adam G., 1976-
    Lantern Sharks / Adam G. Klein.
        p. cm. -- (Sharks. Set II)
    Includes index.
    ISBN 1-59679-287-6
        1. Lantern Sharks--Juvenile literature. I. Title.

QL638.95.D3K58 2005
597.3'6--dc22

                                                    2005040382

CONTENTS

LANTERN SHARKS AND FAMILY

A ghostly glow can be seen deep in the ocean. It appears far beyond where most people travel. Curious fish notice the glow and want to find out more. They have to get closer.

A small fish swims up to the source. But, this is a **dangerous** choice. Behind the glow is a lantern shark. And, it is too late for the fish to escape.

There are about 275 shark species in the world. Like all sharks, lantern sharks are **predatory** fish. All sharks have **cartilage** instead of bones. They also have fins and gills.

The mysteries of the lantern shark are as amazing as its glow. These tiny sharks live deep in the ocean where there is little light. They have adapted unusual ways to survive the cold temperatures and darkness of their **environment**.

This velvet belly lantern shark was found in the Atlantic Ocean in Sogne Fjord, Norway.

WHAT THEY LOOK LIKE

There are more than 45 species of lantern sharks. Even though there are many kinds of them, all lantern sharks share similar **traits**. So, they can be easily identified.

Lantern sharks are dark brown or black. They have long tails. And, there is a large spine in front of each of the two **dorsal** fins on their backs.

DORSAL FIN

CAUDAL (TAIL) FIN

6

PELVIC FIN

Lantern sharks have big eyes. This **trait** is common in deep-sea animals. Lantern sharks also have a flat snout and a small mouth. And, they are covered with tiny scales called **dermal denticles**.

Lantern sharks are some of the smallest sharks on the planet. The dwarf lantern shark is the smallest of the lantern sharks. Adults measure only six to eight inches (15 to 20 cm) long.

Most lantern shark species are about 23 inches (58 cm) long. And like many other sharks, females grow larger than males.

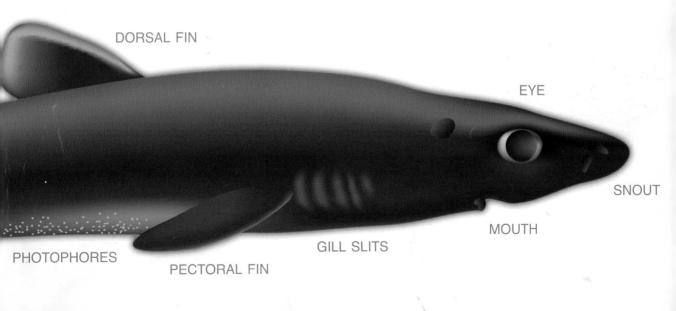

DORSAL FIN

EYE

SNOUT

MOUTH

GILL SLITS

PHOTOPHORES

PECTORAL FIN

WHERE THEY LIVE

Lantern sharks **inhabit** almost every ocean. They are found in the Atlantic Ocean from Scandinavia all the way to South Africa. They live in the deep waters near Japan, Taiwan, and China. They are also found in the South Pacific Ocean and the Mediterranean Sea.

The ocean floor has as much variety as dry land. There are valleys and mountains. There are places with a lot of life and areas that are barren. Temperatures also change from area to area.

Lantern sharks are found between 600 and 3,000 feet (180 and 900 m) under the water's surface. A great lantern shark was even found at about 6,500 feet (2,000 m) deep!

Deep ocean water has unusual features. There is almost no light, which means there are fewer plants. Most deepwater sharks are fairly inactive. So, lantern sharks use less energy than sharks closer to the surface.

But, lantern sharks survive well in these conditions. Their dark bodies blend into their surroundings. And, they have special senses and **traits** that help them stay alive.

Temperature changes lead many shark species to migrate. However, deepwater sharks tend to remain in deeper waters.

Food

Lantern sharks live off of **crustaceans**, smaller fish, and squid. Because these sharks live in deep waters, this food can be scarce. So, lantern sharks use their natural abilities to make finding food easier.

Hunting in the sea is hard work. When hunting, lantern sharks draw their prey out of the darkness with their glowing lights.

Most sharks do not need to eat every day. But lantern sharks eat small prey, so they probably eat more often. It is important for sharks to get the food that they need. Without it they will not have the energy to escape danger or capture another meal.

The lantern shark's large eyes help it see its prey in the dark ocean waters.

SENSES

Recognizing the shape of a lantern shark is a good way to identify one. However, what really makes a lantern shark different is its glow.

On a lantern shark's belly, and sometimes in its mouth, are **organs** called photophores. The photophores give off light by a chemical reaction.

The light the lantern shark gives off is used for finding food and for communicating with other sharks. The light is very important to the lantern shark's survival.

Other senses are vital to sharks. They have good eyesight and a strong sense of smell. They can also sense other animals in the water by the vibrations that the creatures make.

Sharks are able to detect the differences between waves and the movements created by an animal. This can lead a shark to its next meal.

The glow that the lantern shark gives off is called bioluminescence. It is not unique to this shark. Bioluminescence is what makes a firefly glow.

BABIES

Some people believe that the lights on a lantern shark are used to attract a mate. But, there are many unknown things about the mating process. Lantern sharks live so deep in the ocean that it can be difficult to study them.

Female lantern sharks do not lay eggs like many other fish. Instead, they are **ovoviviparous**. The lantern shark's babies remain in the mother even after they hatch. These babies are called pups.

After a short time, the mother gives birth. And, the pups enter the water. The **litter** size varies between species. But, litters of 8 to 24 pups are common for the average lantern shark.

Mother lantern sharks do not take care of their pups after they are birthed. The pups swim off to their new lives as soon as they are born. With luck, they will survive.

A man holds a captured velvet belly lantern shark and an embryo. An embryo is an organism in the early stages of development.

ATTACK AND DEFENSE

Sharks are the most feared sea animal. They normally have few **predators**. In fact, humans and other sharks are their most common enemies.

Unlike many shark species, lantern sharks are not fished commercially. But they are small, so they have many larger sharks to fear.

The lantern shark's dark color helps it remain hidden when necessary. This is its main form of defense against large predators. Another defense is the spines on the lantern shark's back. These sharp spines injure the mouth of the animal that tries to eat it.

Sometimes, predators of the lantern shark come from below. The lantern shark's glow helps it blend into the dim light coming from above.

ATTACKS ON HUMANS

On average, there are 50 shark attacks per year in the world. About six of these are fatal. There are two main reasons why sharks attack humans. The sharks either feel threatened or they are feeding.

A shark can feel threatened for many different reasons. For example, a diver may touch a shark and anger the animal. Or, a surfer may fall in the water and startle a shark.

There are no known cases of lantern sharks attacking humans. This may be because these sharks live at such great depths. So, humans rarely come into contact with them. However, their glow will fascinate humans and other fish for years.

Shark cages protect divers from sharks. The cages also allow humans to learn more about these magnificent creatures while observing them in their natural habitat.

Lantern Shark Facts

Scientific Name:

Luminous shark	*Etmopterus lucifer*
Velvet belly lantern shark	*E. spinax*
Great lantern shark	*E. princeps*
Green lantern shark	*E. virens*
Southern lantern shark	*E. granulosus*
Brown lantern shark	*E. unicolor*
New Zealand lantern shark	*E. baxteri*

Average Size:

23 inches (58 cm)
The dwarf lantern shark is the smallest at six to eight inches (15 to 20 cm) long.

Where They're Found:

Lantern sharks live in deep waters all around the world.

The blackbelly lantern shark is one of the 45 species in the lantern shark family.

GLOSSARY

cartilage (KAHR-tuh-lihj) - the soft, elastic connective tissue in the skeleton. A person's nose and ears are made of cartilage.

crustacean (kruhs-TAY-shuhn) - any of a group of animals with hard shells that live mostly in water. Crabs, lobsters, and shrimps are all crustaceans.

dangerous - able or likely to cause injury or harm.

dermal denticle - a small toothlike projection on a shark's skin.

dorsal - located near or on the back, especially of an animal.

environment - all the surroundings that affect the growth and well-being of a living thing.

inhabit - to live in or occupy a region.

litter - all of the pups born at one time to a mother shark.

organ - a part of an animal or plant that is composed of several kinds of tissues and that performs a specific function. The heart, liver, gallbladder, and intestines are organs of an animal.

ovoviviparous (OH-voh-veye-VIH-puh-ruhs) - a fish or reptile that carries its eggs inside it while they develop.

predator - an animal that kills and eats other animals.

trait - a quality that distinguishes one person or group from another.

WEB SITES

To learn more about lantern sharks, visit ABDO Publishing Company on the World Wide Web at **www.abdopub.com**. Web sites about lantern sharks are featured on our Book Links page. These links are routinely monitored and updated to provide the most current information available.

INDEX